D1516175

THE POCKET LIBRARY OF GREAT ART

Plate 1. SELF-PORTRAIT. *Oil, 1890-95*
Collection Mr. and Mrs. John Hay Whitney, New York

PAUL

GAUGUIN

(1 8 4 8 – 1 9 0 3)

text by

JOHN REWALD

published by HARRY N. ABRAMS, INC., *in association*
with POCKET BOOKS, INC., *New York*

On the cover
TAHITIAN WOMEN WITH MANGO BLOSSOMS
(see color plate 24)

Plate 2. WOMEN AT THE RIVER. *Woodcut, 1891-93*
Museum of Modern Art, New York (Lillie P. Bliss Coll.)

P Gauguin.

The life of Paul Gauguin was so crammed with adventures of all kinds that even a matter-of-fact account cannot decrease its dramatic interest. He was born in Paris in 1848, the year of the second French Revolution; but when reaction took over again a little later, his father, a liberal journalist, had to go into exile. Paul Gauguin was three years old when his parents took him to Peru, the president of that country being a relative of his mother. The child's father died on the voyage, and his mother remained in Lima for only four years. Back in France the boy was raised in Orléans until, at seventeen, he went to sea as an apprentice in the merchant marine and sailed back and forth across the Atlantic Ocean between Rio and Le Havre. After the French defeat in 1871, and the death of his mother, he gave up the sea and took a position in a broker's office in Paris.

For eleven years Gauguin followed a successful business career. In 1873 he married a young Danish girl, leading with her and their children a pleasant, comfortable life. Occasionally, on Sundays, he painted as an amateur, though he was ambitious enough to send a landscape to the Salon of 1876. But, unwilling to follow academic precepts, Gauguin soon began to haunt exhibitions and art galleries. His amazing instinct immediately attracted him to the then still scorned and ridiculed works of the Impressionists, whose canvases he not only admired but also bought. It was not long until he became acquainted with Camille Pissarro, always easy to approach and ready to help beginners. Pissarro introduced him to Cézanne and Degas and arranged for Gauguin to show his timidly Impressionist paintings in the exhibitions of their group in 1880, '81, and '82. His body and soul now consecrated to painting, Gauguin no longer lived except during his hours of liberty from the office. Relying upon his modest savings and his lucky star, he suddenly decided in 1883 to abandon the bank and take up painting "every day." He moved with his wife and five children to Rouen, where Pissarro was then working, but soon found living there too expensive. Madame Gauguin was able to persuade him that an easier life awaited them in Denmark with her relatives. She hoped above all that the insistence of her family would induce her husband to resume his profitable business career. But the sojourn in Copenhagen turned out to be a complete failure. Gauguin was unsuccessful both as a representative for a commercial firm and as an artist. An exhibition of his work was forced to close after only five days.

Discouraged and penniless, Gauguin left his family in

Plate 3. HEAD OF A TAHITIAN WOMAN. *Water color, about 1892*
Collection Mr. and Mrs. Diego Suarez, New York

Plate 4. HUMAN MISERY (MEMORY OF BRITTANY). *Woodcut, 1895-1903*

Copenhagen and returned to Paris in the summer of 1885. He obtained employment as a billposter in Paris railway stations, but ill health forced him to stop work and spend several weeks in a hospital. Yet no misfortune, no poverty, could induce him to abandon his art. Early in 1886 he moved to the small village of Pont-Aven in Brittany, where he found peace, new subjects, and credit at the inn. When he returned to Paris late that same year, he met Vincent van Gogh who greatly admired him.

Overcome by an irresistible desire to escape, Gauguin resolved to leave for Martinique. First he landed in Panama and worked as a common laborer with the diggers of the Panama Canal, to earn his passage to the island. He immediately fell in love with the exotic beauty of Martinique and infused his Impressionist work with some of its tropical colors. But, unable to endure the climate, he obtained passage home as a sailor and late in 1887 returned to France, sick and exhausted. Once more he went to live in Pont-Aven, where he soon met a young friend of Van Gogh's, Emile Bernard. Under his influence, he now gradually broke away from Impressionism and adopted a bolder style, somewhat inspired by Japanese prints, with radical simplifications of drawing, brilliant, pure, bright colors, an ornamental character of composition, and willful flatness of planes—a style which he called Synthetism.

At the insistence of Vincent van Gogh, and with the financial help of Vincent's brother Theo, Gauguin left Pont-Aven in the fall of 1888 to join Van Gogh in Arles. But their divergent temperaments and opinions soon caused the two friends to quarrel violently. Van Gogh suffered a nervous breakdown, followed by an attack of insanity during which he threatened Gauguin's life. After Van Gogh had been taken in a serious condition to the public hospital in Arles, Gauguin left hurriedly for Paris, and thence again for Brittany.

Plate 5. THE NIGHTMARE. *Monotype, about 1892*
Wildenstein and Co., New York

Gauguin's new style attracted the attention of several young painters in Pont-Aven and he slowly gathered a small group of followers around him. Yet this modest success was not accompanied by any material benefits. The dreariness of his situation once more stirred in Gauguin the irresistible desire to seek out faraway lands, despite the failure of his trip to Martinique. At the end of 1890, he went back to Paris to prepare for a voyage to Tahiti, dreaming of life under palm trees and a tropical sun.

Living in the jungle of Tahiti, Gauguin set out to work feverishly, his imagination tremendously stimulated by his lovely and peaceful surroundings. His will to simplify forms as well as his arbitrary use of colors, combined with his literary aspirations, gave his work its decorative stamp. Thus the novelty of Gauguin's art consisted not only in his subjects, but also in his conception of these subjects, in his efforts to reconcile the barbarous character of Maori idols with the sensitivity of a European artist.

After the first few months in Tahiti, Gauguin's enthusiasm was once more supplanted by bitter resignation; hunger and poverty again became his daily guests. He fell ill and spat alarming quantities of blood. Finally, in desperation, he begged to be taken home. The French government repatriated him in the summer of 1893. In Paris unexpected news awaited him: an uncle in Orléans had left him a small legacy, and Gauguin was able to spend money liberally, if only for a short while. He held a comprehensive exhibition which met with little success, rented a large studio where he lived with an Indonesian girl, gave receptions, and undertook some short trips, including one to Copenhagen. He spent the summer of 1894 once more in Pont-Aven, accompanied by his young mistress. Some slighting remarks addressed to the strange couple involved him in a brawl with several sailors during which his ankle was broken.

During his sleepless nights Gauguin now again aban-

Plate 6. STANDING EVE. *Drawing, about 1891-93*
Wildenstein and Co., New York

doned himself to his favorite dream: life in the tropics. In spite of his harassing experiences, of hunger and illness suffered in the South Seas, he decided to return there, this time forever. Disposing of everything he owned at public auction (though he had to buy back most of his pictures so as not to let them go for ridiculous prices), Gauguin got ready to leave in the spring of 1895.

The fate that awaited him in Tahiti was no more pleasant than the one he had met there before. He worked only between trips to the hospital, accumulated debts, was grief-stricken at the news of the death of his favorite child. Eventually in 1898 he went to hide himself in the mountains and attempted suicide, but unsuccessfully; even death did not want him. Meanwhile in Paris the dealer Ambroise Vollard began to take some interest in Gauguin's work, exhibited his paintings and offered him a contract which guaranteed him at least the bare essentials of his frugal life. But now the painter began to quarrel with the colonial administration until, after several more sojourns at the hospital, he sold his belongings in 1901 and left Tahiti for the nearby island of Hiva-Hoa.

Gauguin began to think of returning to France when his health improved and he was able to paint more frequently. However, he still suffered from heart trouble and from eczema of his injured foot. Whenever he could not paint, he wrote his memoirs as well as acid letters to various local officials, one of whom brought suit against him. In January 1903, a cyclone destroyed his hut; in March he was condemned to several weeks in prison and found himself without means to go to Tahiti for an appeal. Yet no appeal was necessary. The threat of imprisonment released him to death. Gauguin expired on May 8, 1903, lonely and heartbroken, far from his country, his family, his friends. But ever since, his paintings have asserted his powerful presence throughout the civilized world.

Plate 7. SEATED WOMAN *(study for color plate 25)*
Monotype, about 1902. Private Collection, New York

Plate 8. SEATED WOMAN. *Terra cotta, about 1890*
Wildenstein and Co., New York

COLOR PLATES

PLATE 9

Painted 1888

STILL LIFE WITH PUPPIES

Museum of Modern Art, New York
(Mrs. Simon Guggenheim Fund)
32⅝ x 21⅝"

During the summer of 1888 Gauguin and his young friend Emile Bernard, with whom he was working in Pont-Aven, Brittany, expressed the intention to "paint like children." Yet—far from the true primitiveness that expressed itself so touchingly in the works of the *douanier* Rousseau—Gauguin's approach to his subjects was a highly reasoned one, a conscious attempt to simplify forms and colors for the benefit of a more striking expression. He now was also inclined to eliminate shadows because they represent a realistic approach. Shadows are indeed absent from this strange still life, painted on a large wooden panel. It shows three little pinkish-gray puppies, three deep blue goblets, and some fruit assembled with an utter disregard for proportion or natural coloration. In all probability this is one of Gauguin's attempts to paint "like children," an attempt which shows him far ahead of his time.

PLATE 10

Painted 1888

BRETON PEASANT WOMEN

Bavarian State Painting Collections, Munich

28¼ x 35¾"

In 1888 Gauguin abandoned his Impressionist style and
adopted his Synthetist form of expression. His canvas
of *Breton Peasant Women* is typical evidence of this
evolution. The colors are still rather soft; they were
soon to become much more outspoken and clashing.
The brush strokes are still reminiscent of gentle Impressionist hatchings, which favor delicate gradations
of tone; they were soon to be replaced by large flat
planes of uniform color. The composition, however,
already shows a concern with decorative patterns that
was alien to the Impressionists.

Gauguin at first appears to have been attracted by
the idyllic quality of Breton landscapes and the pic-
turesque costumes of the peasants. It was only somewhat
later that his will to stylize prompted him to turn his
back more and more on the amiable aspects of Brittany, in order to emphasize the savageness of its nature
and the mysticism of its inhabitants which he discovered
beneath its lovely appearance.

PLATE II

Painted 1889

THE YELLOW CHRIST

Albright Art Gallery, Buffalo

36¼ x 28¾"

In *The Yellow Christ* Gauguin exemplifies his newly developed theory that the impression of nature must be wedded to the aesthetic sentiment which chooses, arranges, simplifies, and synthesizes; the painter ought not to rest until he has given birth to the child of his imagination, begotten in a union of his mind with reality. "Don't copy nature too much," he wrote from Brittany to a friend. "Art is an abstraction; derive this abstraction from nature while dreaming in front of it, but think more of creating than of the actual result."

In *The Yellow Christ*—inspired by the crude stone crucifixes to be found on the waysides in Brittany— Gauguin felt free to use the elements of nature which best suited his purpose; and in this picture his purpose was, as he himself said, to convey the "great rustic and *superstitious* simplicity" which struck him among the peasant folk. Reducing all forms to their essential outlines, using pure colors, avoiding shadows and modeling, he attained in this work a strange eloquence, a mixture of crudeness and subtlety.

Plate 12. THE SWINEHERD, BRITTANY *(commentary follows color pl*

PLATE 13

Painted 1890

PORTRAIT OF A WOMAN

The Art Institute of Chicago
(Winterbotham Collection)

24½ x 20¼"

Untiringly Gauguin proclaimed his admiration for Cézanne, an admiration shared by all of his friends, particularly Emile Bernard. Gauguin had met Cézanne through Pissarro in 1881 and had become the owner of several of his paintings. When circumstances forced him to dispose of his collection, assembled in the affluent days of his bank job, there was one canvas with which he refused to part: a still life by Cézanne. He apparently carried it with him wherever he went, for he must have had it in Brittany when he painted this *Portrait of a Woman,* which is supposed to represent Marie Henry, owner of the small inn at Le Pouldu where Gauguin lived in 1889 and 1890. Indeed, in the background of this portrait Gauguin copied his Cézanne still life, a silent tribute to his "master" as well as an eloquent confirmation that during all his searching, painting, and theorizing in Brittany, Cézanne's example was always vividly before his eyes.

Painted 1891

WE GREET THEE, MARY

(Ia Orana Maria)

The Metropolitan Museum of Art, New York
(Lewisohn Collection)

44¾ x 34½"

In Brittany Gauguin had been greatly impressed by the devoutness of the peasants and had painted several pictures of biblical or religious subjects, such as *The Yellow Christ* (plate 11). During his first sojourn in Tahiti he was inspired to paint yet another religious canvas, *We Greet Thee, Mary,* in which he used the tropical setting for a biblical scene.

Early in 1892 Gauguin wrote to a friend: "I have painted a canvas: an angel with yellow wings who points out to two Tahitian women the figures of Mary and Jesus, also Tahitians. In the background somber mountains and flowering trees. A dark purple road and an emerald green foreground. I am rather satisfied with it."

This painting has all the tenderness of genuine religious emotion, combined with the exotic elements that had drawn the artist to the tropical island: the beauty of its women, the splendor of its vegetation, and the mysticism of the natives.

IA ORANA MARIA

Painted 1891

TAHITIAN LANDSCAPE

Minneapolis Institute of Arts

26¾ x 36⅜"

Once he had abandoned Impressionism, Gauguin painted very few pure landscapes as he had done before under Pissarro's guidance. It would seem that in Tahiti the natives attracted him almost more than the beautiful scenery, or at least that he seldom contemplated this scenery without simultaneously thinking of its inhabitants who, in his mind, were an inseparable part of it. Their strange customs, their nimble bodies, their colorful raiment deeply stirred his imagination. Yet every now and then he let himself be impregnated with the mystic charm of a tropical landscape such as this, where he studied nature almost without thinking of its inhabitants; the lone native and the black animal hardly interfere with the majesty of the scene—they even appear to accentuate its solitude.

ENTIRE PAINTING ABOVE
LIFT FOLD FOR DETAIL

PLATE 17

Painted 1891

STILL LIFE WITH FLOWERS

Collection Mr. and Mrs. Edward G. Robinson,
Beverly Hills, California

37¼ x 24½"

Together with landscapes, still lifes had played an important role in Gauguin's early years as a painter. In Tahiti he apparently was less tempted by them, but he succumbed from time to time to the enchantment of sparkling bouquets rich in shapes and colors unknown to the European gardener. He assembled these exotic flowers in earthen pots which he made himself and delighted in depicting their freshness and glory. If there is still an echo of Cézanne's influence, there is also, in the sumptuousness of the coloration, a hint of Redon's magic pastels of flowers. (Gauguin had met Redon shortly before leaving for Tahiti and had received one of his works which he had taken with him.) But while Redon often invented the forms of his lovely blossoms, Gauguin remained closer to nature, which offered him such enticing models. Here he could use color freely and establish lively contrasts which seemed governed by sheer hazard, though his bouquets were arranged with loving care.

PLATE 18

Painted 1892

WORDS OF THE DEVIL

(Parau Nà Te Varua Ino)

Collection Mr. and Mrs. W. Averell Harriman, New York

36¾ x 27¾"

The words "mysterious" and "enigmatic" often appear
in Gauguin's letters and notes; indeed these were qual-
ities which struck him, the European, so particularly
among the South Sea people. And frequently he tried
to capture in his works this element of an impenetrable
world hidden behind the friendliness, the unconcern,
even the apparent openness of the natives.

"She is very clever in her naïveté, the Tahitian Eve,"
Gauguin once wrote. "Like Eve's, her body is still that
of an animal, but the mind has developed subtlety, love
impressed the ironical smile upon her lips, and naïvely
she searches in her memory for the *why* of present times.
Enigmatically she looks at you."

That Gauguin succeeded in capturing this enigmatic
character is illustrated by the exclamation of Mallarmé
before one of these Tahitian paintings: "It is amazing
that one can put so much mystery in so much brilliance."

Plate 19. WHISPERED WORDS *(commentary follows color plate sectio*

PLATE 20

Painted 1893

THE MOON AND THE EARTH

(Hina Te Fatou)

Museum of Modern Art, New York

44½ x 24"

Towards the end of his life Gauguin endeavored to explain the origin of paintings such as this, based not so much on scenes observed as on a peculiar mixture of things seen and imagined.

"Here near my cabin," he wrote, "in complete silence, amid the intoxicating perfumes of nature, I dream of violent harmonies. A delight enhanced by I know not what sacred horror I divine in the infinite. Animal figures rigid as statues, with something indescribably solemn and religious in the rhythm of their pose, in their strange immobility. In eyes that dream, the troubled surface of an unfathomable enigma. ∴ . . I have tried to interpret my vision in an appropriate décor and with all the simplicity the medium permits."

When Gauguin returned to Paris in 1893, he exhibited this painting, together with *We Greet Thee, Mary* (plate 14) and *Words of the Devil* (plate 18), in his one-man show. Before he left again in 1895, it was sold at auction and acquired by Degas.

Painted 1896

NATIVITY

(*Te Tamari No Atua*)

Bavarian State Painting Collections, Munich

37¼ x 50¾"

In July, 1895, Gauguin returned to Tahiti after an absence of almost two years during which he had plunged himself once more into the agitated life of Paris. This time he had tried to sell everything he owned, leaving France forever. During the summer of 1896 he proudly informed a friend that Tahiti was beautiful and that his new "wife" was named Pahura and was fourteen years old. There can be little doubt that in his canvas of the *Nativity,* painted that same year, the young mother is none but Pahura and that the child held by the woman behind her is Gauguin's own.

If, in *We Greet Thee, Mary* (plate 14), Gauguin transposed a biblical scene into a tropical setting, he seems here to have reversed the process, turning a native scene into a biblical one. Were it not for the faint halos that surround the heads of the recumbent woman and of the child, this painting might well be considered a colorful and poetic interpretation of an aspect of South Sea life.

ENTIRE PAINTING ABOVE
◄— LIFT FOLD FOR DETAIL

PLATE 23

Painted 1898

THE WHITE HORSE

The Louvre, Paris

$55\frac{1}{2} \times 35\frac{3}{4}''$

This painting illustrates particularly well the peculiar fashion in which Gauguin combined the flat pattern and asymmetrical composition of Japanese prints with an execution derived from the Impressionists and a palette rich in exotic colors and contrasts. He painted this work with vivid brush strokes (occasionally using a palette knife) applied on a coarse canvas, the rough texture of which adds to its mysterious savagery.

The diagonal branches provide the arabesque that pulls together the various large planes of more or less uniform colors. Against these flat areas, which give the landscape an abstract character, appear the horses and their riders treated in a three-dimensional way, with shadows carefully modeling their forms. Yet contrasts of colors, lines, and forms are well integrated, leading the eye from the white flower in the right corner to the curved lines of the horse and across the meandering branches into an undefined distance.

PLATE 24

Painted 1899

TAHITIAN WOMEN
WITH MANGO BLOSSOMS

The Metropolitan Museum of Art, New York
(W. C. Osborn Collection)

37 x 28¾"

Throughout the nineteenth century, French painters strove to discover new types of feminine beauty or even —in some cases—of ugliness. Ingres established the cold perfection of virginal nudes; Delacroix proclaimed the enticing loveliness of oriental odalisques; Courbet chose the carnal flamboyance of heavy-set models; Puvis de Chavannes paid homage to the classical beauty of Arcadian women; Renoir rediscovered the voluptuous charm of buxom girls; Seurat painted his slim models with no trace of sensuality; Degas preferred the angular and not yet fully developed bodies of young dancers, whom he presented without flattery; and Lautrec went even further, selecting his models among prostitutes and painting them with a cruel insistence on their depravity. But Gauguin dreamed of exotic loveliness and went all the way to the South Seas attracted by an entirely different type of beauty, chaste and yet sensuous, dark bodies full of promise, large eyes full of mystery. Here he found Eve in an untroubled paradise, not knowing the meaning of sin.

DETAIL OF COVER PLATE

PLATE 25

Painted 1902

THE CALL

(L'Appel)

The Cleveland Museum of Art (Gift of Hanna Fund)

51¼ x 35½"

Whenever he detached himself somewhat from his literary inspirations and dreams, Gauguin conceived paintings which seem based more closely on his observations of daily life in the tropical islands. *Whispered Words* (plate 19) is one of these canvases, *The Call* is yet another. Here the artist makes less frequent use of the ornamental elements and flat patterns which appear in more imaginary works like *The Moon and the Earth* (plate 20) or *The White Horse* (plate 23). Instead, he strives for a more naturalistic representation, using small brush strokes which model forms and indicate textures, and his color harmonies are softer. He avoids the sharp contrasts which he favors elsewhere when he wants to create a dreamlike atmosphere. What the composition loses in mystery it gains in quiet grandeur and peace. Forgetting his worries and sufferings, the artist finds here a happy expression of the nature and the people he so deeply loved.

Painted 1899

ON THE BEACH, TAHITI

(Te Tini Nave Ite Rata)

Private Collection, Buffalo

29 x 37"

Gauguin liked to quote what Degas had once said of him, comparing him to the wolf of La Fontaine's fable who—although he would prefer as good and easy a life as that led by the well-fed dog—chooses hardship rather than wear a collar, a collar that would enslave him.

If Gauguin thought of Puvis de Chavannes in Tahiti (and his letters and notes prove that he frequently did), then this idyllic landscape is a good illustration of the different approach of the two painters. Gauguin himself has expressed it in these words: "Puvis explains his idea, yes, but he doesn't paint it. He is Greek, whereas I am a savage, a wolf of the forest without a collar. Puvis would entitle a painting *Purity* and, to explain the title, would paint a young virgin with a lily in her hand—a well-known symbol, understood by everybody. Gauguin, under the title *Purity,* will paint a landscape with limpid waters unsullied by civilized man; maybe one figure."

ENTIRE PAINTING ABOVE
◄— LIFT FOLD FOR DETAIL

PLATE 2 8

Painted 1897

WHERE DO WE COME FROM? WHAT ARE WE?
WHERE ARE WE GOING?

Museum of Fine Arts, Boston

55½ x 148¼"

In December, 1897, Gauguin had felt unable to stand any longer the life of intermittent sickness and increasing debts he was leading in Tahiti. He resolved to kill himself, but before doing so he decided to draw upon all his remaining strength to paint a last important composition. He has told in great detail the story of this work:

"Before I died I wished to paint a large canvas that I had in mind, and I worked day and night that whole month in an incredible fever. Of course it is not done like a Puvis de Chavannes: studies after nature, then preparatory sketches, etc. It is all done from imagination, straight from the brush on a coarse sackcloth full of knots, and the appearance is terribly rough. . . . I am looking at it all the time and (I'll admit) I admire it. The more I look at it, the more I realize its enormous mathematical faults, but I would not retouch them for anything. The painting must remain as it is—merely a sketch, if one wishes."

◄— LIFT FOLD FOR ENTIRE PAINTING

Painted 1897

WHERE DO WE COME FROM? WHAT ARE WE? WHERE ARE WE GOING?

Gauguin has given the following description of this large canvas: "To the right, in the lower corner [see detail opposite], a sleeping child and three seated women. Two figures dressed in purple confide their thoughts to one another. An enormous crouching figure [see detail, plate 30], out of all proportion, and intentionally so, raises its arm and stares in astonishment upon these two who dare think of their destiny. A figure in the center is picking fruit. Two cats near a child. A white goat. An idol, its arms mysterious and rhythmically raised, seems to indicate the Beyond. A seated girl [Gauguin's "wife," Pahura] seems to listen to the idol. Lastly, an old woman nearing death appears to accept everything, to resign herself to her thoughts. She completes the story. At her feet a strange white bird . . . represents the futility of words. The scene is on the bank of a small river in the woods. In the background the ocean and beyond it the mountains of a neighboring island."

Painted 1897

WHERE DO WE COME FROM? WHAT ARE WE?
WHERE ARE WE GOING?

After completing this monumental composition, Gauguin
went into the mountains to commit suicide. However,
the dose of arsenic he took apparently was too strong;
vomiting counteracted the effects of the poison. After
a night of terrible suffering he returned home. (There
is no mention of Pahura in Gauguin's accounts of his
suicide attempt, though she shared his life from 1896
to 1901.)

When Gauguin sent this painting to Paris, where it
was shown at Vollard's in 1898, the critic A. Fontainas
commented: "In the large panel by Gauguin there is
nothing that explains the meaning of the allegory." The
painter thereupon wrote a lengthy reply: "Yes, there
is: my dream is intangible, it comprises no allegory;
as Mallarmé said, 'It is a musical poem, it needs no
libretto.' Consequently the essence of a work, unsub-
stantial and out of reach, consists precisely of 'that
which is not expressed; it flows by implication from the
lines without color or words; it is not a material
structure.' "

PLATE 3 1

Painted 1902

CONTES BARBARES

Folkwang Museum, Essen

51¼ x 35½"

Among the many Maori women whom Gauguin painted, this young girl with the strange red hair stands out for her particular sweetness, beauty, and grace. Indeed, she reminded his friend Morice of Botticelli, and this seems not unwarranted, since Gauguin greatly admired Botticelli and had a photograph of one of his paintings in his room in Brittany. But, as if to offset the loveliness of these two nudes—and also as if to recapture another memory of Brittany—Gauguin introduced into the composition the rather hideous features of a man with clawed feet, presumably the one who evokes before the two girls the barbaric tales of their mythology. His head is the exact repetition of a portrait which Gauguin had painted in 1889 of his friend and patron Meyer de Haan (see plate 34), a dwarfed Dutch painter with whom he had worked in Brittany and who originally had intended to accompany the artist to the South Seas. Thus this painting combines in a strange way the enchanting youth of the tropics with the ugliness of the old world.

Painted 1888

THE SWINEHERD, BRITTANY

Collection Mrs. James Fosburgh, New York

29 x 36½"

Throughout 1888 and 1889 Gauguin seems to have done a number of paintings of an experimental character. Sometimes he relied mostly on an Impressionist execution but used very vivid colors; sometimes he worked with flat planes and accentuated outlines, as Emile Bernard did; and sometimes he combined both techniques. In this large and important Breton landscape with a young swineherd, he abandoned crude simplifications, strong colors, and flat areas for little brush strokes, soft harmonies, and small patches well integrated into the composition. While the scene does not seem to represent any specific place in Brittany, it appears to synthesize all the quiet charm and colorful greatness of the landscape that had captivated Gauguin. Yet even here we find an insistence on line and a summarization of forms that show a definite step beyond Impressionism, in spite of the execution which, unlike the *Still Life with Puppies* (plate 9), features a texture of small strokes.

Painted 1892

WHISPERED WORDS

(Parau-Parau)

Collection Mr. and Mrs. John Hay Whitney, New York

30 x 38"

Among the many notes on his life and work which Gauguin jotted down in the loneliness of his hut in Tahiti, there is a passage that seems to have been written almost specifically for this painting, though it treats his exotic art in general:

"As I want to suggest an exuberant and wild nature and a tropical sun which sets on fire everything around it, I have to give my figures an appropriate frame. It really is open-air life, although intimate; in the thickets and the shaded brooks, those whispering women in an immense palace decorated by nature itself with all the riches that Tahiti holds. Hence these fabulous colors and this fiery, yet softened and silent air."

Plate 32. BRETON WOMAN. *Pastel, 1886-88*
Glasgow Art Galleries, Scotland (Burrell Collection)

Plate 33. GIRL WITH FOX. *Chalk, about 1891*
Collection Mr. and Mrs. Leigh B. Block, Chicago

Plate 34. MEYER DE HAAN. *Water color, about 1890*
Wildenstein and Co., New York

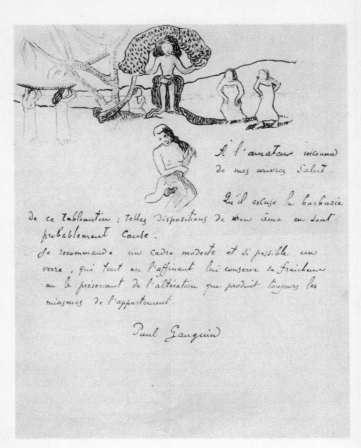

À l'amateur inconnu
de mes œuvres Salut.

Qu'il excuse la barbarie
de ce tableautin ; telles dispositions de mon âme en sont
probablement cause.

Je recommande un cadre modeste et si possible un
verre , qui tout en l'affinant lui conserve sa fraicheur
en le préservant de l'altération que produit toujours les
miasmes de l'appartement.

Paul Gauguin

Plate 35. LETTER WITH ILLUSTRATIONS. *Ink, 1896*
Collection Mr. and Mrs. Alex Lewyt, New York

Plate 36. TAHITIAN FAMILY. *Monotype, 1895-1903*
Private Collection, France

Plate 37. GIRL WITH DEVIL. *Monotype, 1895-1903*
Private Collection, France

Plate 38. SOYEZ MYSTERIEUSES. *Colored wood bas-relief, 1890. Form*

Plate 39. TAHITIAN WOMEN *(study for color plate 25)*
Drawing, 1902. Private Collection, France

Plate 40. CHANGE OF RESIDENCE. *Monotype, 1895-1903*
    Private Collection, France

Plate 41. SELF-PORTRAIT. *Plaster bas-relief*
Formerly Collection A. Schuffenecker, Paris

BIOGRAPHICAL NOTES

1848 Paul Gauguin (pronounced *Go-GAN*) born in Paris on June 7.

1851 Leaves with parents for Lima, Peru, where mother has relatives. Father dies on trip.

1855–64 Returns with mother; school years in Orléans.

1865–71 Serves in merchant marine and French Navy; quits Navy after mother dies, works in Paris bank.

1873 Marries Danish Mette Gad.

1874–79 Takes interest in art; collects Impressionist paintings and begins to paint on Sundays. Exhibits for the first time at Salon of 1876. Works with Pissarro at Pontoise in 1879.

1880–83 Exhibits in fifth, sixth, and seventh Impressionist shows; meets and admires Cézanne. Quits bank job for painting.

1884–85 Moves to Rouen (where Pissarro works); joins wife's family in Copenhagen, but returns with one of his five children to Paris, where he earns meager livelihood as poster-hanger.

1886 Exhibits in last Impressionist show. First stay in Pont-Aven, Brittany, where he meets Emile Bernard. Friendship with Van Gogh.

1887 Leaves for Martinique; works on Panama Canal. Returns to France in December.

Plate 42. OVIRI THE SAVAGE. *Terra cotta, about 1891-93*
Private Collection, France

1888	Works with Emile Bernard in Pont-Aven. Joins Van Gogh in Arles but leaves after violent quarrels and Van Gogh's breakdown.
1889–90	Organizes "Synthetist" exhibition at Paris World's Fair. Lives in Brittany; returns to Paris late in 1890 to leave for Tahiti.
1891	Auctions his paintings to raise money for trip; leaves Paris in April, arrives in Papeete in June and settles in wilderness.
1893	Sick and in debt, returns to France in August and receives small inheritance from uncle. Rents Paris studio; shows at Durand-Ruel's.
1894	Short visit to Copenhagen, spends most of year in Brittany. Breaks ankle in brawl with sailor.
1895	Decides to return to Tahiti. After second auction sale, leaves Paris and arrives in Papeete in July; again settles away from city.
1896–97	Repeated illness, sojourns at hospital, increasing debts; lives with Pahura, a girl of fourteen.
1898	Attempts suicide.
1900	Contract with Vollard. Back in hospital.
1901	Moves to Atuana on Dominique Island in the Marquesas; Pahura refuses to accompany him.
1902	Ill again, considers return to France.
1903	Cyclone ravages the island. After quarrels with the authorities, is condemned to three months' imprisonment and fine for writing letter of complaint. Dies in Atuana, May 8.

SOME OTHER BOOKS
ABOUT GAUGUIN

Robert Burnett. *The Life of Paul Gauguin*. London, Cobden-Sanderson, 1936

Paul Gauguin. *Intimate Journals*. New York, Crown Publishers, 1936

Paul Gauguin. *Letters to Georges Daniel de Monfreid*. New York, Dodd, Mead, 1922

Paul Gauguin. *Letters to His Wife and Friends*. Cleveland, World, 1948

Pola Gauguin. *My Father, Paul Gauguin*. New York, Alfred A. Knopf, 1937

Maurice Malingue. *Gauguin*. Monaco, Les Documents d'Art, 1944

John Rewald. *Gauguin*. New York, Hyperion, 1938

Jean de Rotonchamp. *Paul Gauguin*. Paris, Crès, 1925

ACKNOWLEDGMENTS

In a book of art, it seems particularly fitting to acknowledge the work of craftsmen who contribute to its making. The color plates were made by Litho-Art, Inc., New York. The lithography is from the presses of The Meehan-Tooker Co., Inc., New York and the binding has been done by F. M. Charlton Co., New York. The paper was made by P. H. Glatfelter Co., Spring Grove, Pa. Our deepest indebtedness is to the museums, galleries, and private collectors who graciously permitted the reproduction of their paintings, drawings, and sculpture.